Our Hope Remains

OUR

AN ANTHOLOGY

Our Hope Remains: An Anthology Vol. 1

Copyright © 2023 Acclivity Publishing

ISBN-13: 979-8-218-12209-6

Acclivity Publishing

Cover & Interior Design
Acclivity Publishing

Edited by Acclivity Publishing

ACCLIVITY
PUBLISHING

To the afraid
&
the uncertain

-

the brave
&
the hopeful.

Thank you for never giving up hope.

CONTENTS

CONTENTS

CONTENTS

CONTENTS

CONTENTS

We often use the word "hope" with a casual or general wondering if something will or will not occur such as "I hope today will be a good day," or "I hope everything works out." In fact, we almost attribute hope to a fleeting feeling.

Hope according to God's Word denotes expectation and security. It paints the picture of excited anticipation that the promises which have been given are steadfast and sure.

Hope is often the conduit by which we feel peace, happiness, and security. It's having full assurance that our current tribulations and hardships have an outcome that will work out in our favor. It's for this reason that I believe hope is one of the primary driving forces for living.

This anthology is an endeavor by 9 poets, from different walks of life from around the world. Their collective works are those that reflect their view of hope in these current times. Through love, loss, brokenness, injustice and fear, these writers have eloquently painted a picture of assurance through poetry.

These are words for those who wait.
These are words for you.

The world of poetry is vast, diverse, unabashed and often uninhibited. The poet is able to meld elements of meter, verse, flow, imagery and allegory to present to their audience something profound.

When considering a piece, understand that each poet has a unique voice and method of delivering their message. Poetry is an art-form, and therefore each 'voice' is uniquely expressive both in performance and on paper.

Both traditional and contemporary poets have come together within the pages of this anthology, each to present ideas for you and I to extrapolate. You'll find a diverse, yet unified message of perseverance from the words of these poets on every page.

Knowing this, it may help to be aware of the following:
1. Consider each poet's point of view.
2. Read the poem slowly and if you want, out loud.
3. Read it twice and explore the emotions it evokes.
4. Consider the meaning beyond the poet's choice of punctuation or capitalization.
5. Sound and rhythm are intentional in poetry.
6. Some poets utilize line-breaks and enjambment for impact and... some do not!

So that's it! We believe you'll find some encouragement within these pages, and with careful consideration, discover we've got a lot in common.

EDWARD HOLMES
ANTHOLOGY POET

Edward L. Holmes II is an American poet, spoken word artist and author with an evangelist's tongue and a heart for the hurting.

Today he is passionate about producing consistent, quality non-fiction that motivates, uplifts and educates. With an addicted and broken life-altered by his faith on the forefront, Edward believes in practical theology and instilling hope into every open mic and heart.

His writing style is a mix of versed and free form poetry steeped in hope, healing and honesty.

 # WHAT IS HOPE?

It's the ability to press forward into the unknown with the unshakable expectation that everything is going to be alright. End of story.

 # I WRITE BECAUSE...

Earth has no shortage of broken hearts. With words at our disposal, I believe conscious writers have a mission. Words have the power to reach the human soul, and for that reason alone, I refuse to stop writing.

Brave

What is the definition?
We are told, it's the heart that's bold, but
are we missing something bigger?
I sat up one night pondering the meaning
wondering, receding
deeper into definitions
of a destination not obtained.
12 A.M. met my sleepless sight
perseverating over percolated liquid life
that night. Would the bottom of the red-eye
give me insight? Is it confidence, assuredness,
a man fearless enough to pass the test?
I digress,
wrestling with unrest over the concept of
this.

Yet, all I can conclude is that, even though we
are taught to believe that reckless abandon
goes hand in hand with what it means to be brave,
this is not at all what I've seen to be true...

It's the young mind riddled with suicide inside
who tried life one more time today.
It's the assault survivor that still
holds onto the concept of love and purity.
It's the single mother who provides
for the lives of her children in the midst of poverty.
It's the father who stays,
the sister who prays,
beloved, these are the brave.

Salt

I was nearly skeptical of You as I stood
in a hot tear-soaked suit coat during
Sunday service. Her words with
trembling lips ripped holes like bullets
through my chest
as she tried her best to
question this mess of a man,
who at the time seemed prepared to answer
to the pervasive cancer of abuse.

"Why would *He* let them do this to me?"
Her words quivered, questioning sovereignty.

   I had no reply.
      For even I wondered as well.

   No reply,
   but tears *for* you.
         With you.
Beloved, tears were all that we had.
No prophetic pomp of oil-drenched
petition to peace that for a rift in time
we couldn't feel.

But we can cry.

Child of God, drench the road you walk.
Don't hold back,
but from the belly, baby, bellow,
and let the Hoover Dam
of every ignorant "hush, baby, hush" gush forth,
silencing the monsters who mute you.

Answers will come in time,
but today...
today
we can cry.

Mercy Runs

She is wild like the flowers
in her hair, seemingly impervious
to destruction and unshakable like
the fortress she built.

The elements stop to ruminate
on her words, rain bows at her strength while
thunder claps at her innumerable victories
that command such undying attention.

She is cloaked in broken hopes and
chosen, chose sin, yet flows in gifts when needed.
She pleaded to be whole, while holding onto
that pride she possessed, which eventually needed to fall.

Through valleys, hills, deserts, seas &
seasons, mercy sees into
the strongholds of her heart which
couldn't keep her captive much longer.

The fortress she built
that commanded such undying attention;
that pride she possessed, which eventually needed to fall
couldn't keep her captive much longer.

Lion's Tooth

Sometimes
weather-worn sidewalks give birth to
dandelions seeded in earthen wombs of
impossible circumstances.
No matter how arduous the journey,
she will continue to dream
and grow
    and grow
       and grow
until her prowess is pronounced;
pushing her past proverbial prohibitions
of her petrifying past before illumination,
and with her head held high, she will
praise the sun.

Dirt was her covering,
but never her definition.
Her mission is far too brilliant,
she is far too resilient
to be silenced.

Bloom is what she was created to do.
Bloom is what she will.

Focus

I've seen broken people in
a million different places,
broken hearts behind the smiles
on a multitude of faces.

Men are masking mangled memories
in all the broken spaces of the places
fear erased the hope
disparity replaces.

How I pray these broken brothers
with their burdens and their woes
could find the missing peace they've lost
within their troubled souls.

By now you might be wondering
how one can see the truth.
Darling, you can spot the broken folk if
you've been broken too.

That Day

Until every tear is wiped away and forgotten
as though the salt of sorrow
never streaked the cheek, I'll speak of hope
that soaks and saturates those who wait.

Until you and I are unified in glory
and our story concludes. Until they see my
black boy blood bleeds the same hue as you.
With no barriers we'll be carriers of hope in You.

Until the concept of expiration itself expires
under the foot of the Lamb, the I AM
who stands with authority over death in his hands.
We can walk hopeful in vicarious victory and liberty.

Until that day...

Until that day I pray we stay steadfast in hope.

Until that day...

Until that day...

Over My Head

You're not shaken,
forsaken or left to die,
overtaken by life's turbulent tide,
choking through the blow of the undertow.

> Know that coming back to shore at times
> takes emergency measures to rescue you
> from personal pride and pleasures.
> Hold your breath, son
> God's not done.

Blameless

It's not your fault,
but for so long you've heard it from
everyone else that you started to believe it.
People make choices
and hurting *you*
was theirs.

You've been trying to
wash away stains that you were never
strong enough to clean.
You were created to be spotless
and that job
      is His.

Roads Less Traveled

It's commonplace to sour the face,
then pout and talk about
the problematic lives we live than
wear a smile.

So wear a bright visage
that shines and shows appreciation
for the life we get to live amidst
our trials.

It's true this world has many woes
and pain will never falter
while it's showing us how easily
we b r e a k.

So, grin and grimace greatly
even when your hope's escaping
and you'll see that trials,
a stronger man,
will make.

I Dropped My Shame Along the Way

"I don't need anyone else," I said to myself.
It was already a quarter past midnight, streets
shimmering to the cadence of the rain.
Pain still filled my selfish will while guilt pushed two feet
as far as they could carry me.
from You.

"I'm fine on my own," I said, alone,
walking past illuminated homes. Knowing I had only
been shown unending kindness,
my mess made of mindless ambitions clouded my sight
that night keeping my heart
from You.

"I've no regrets," I said, cold and wet,
down streetlight-lined sidewalks towards the gate.
This late,
no one would wait
for me to be safe, so why stay anyway?
My shame and I; the renegade and runaway
from You.

"I can't see home from here..."
                stopping,
                        sobbing,
                                trembling,
nothing near to me resembling anything reminiscent
of home, yet hearing one familiar tone
of voice behind my back,
to remind me of this very simple fact:
"Son, you can't flee far enough from My arms."

And I dropped my shame along the way back.

Why the Kettle Sings

I'm convinced...
    that God loves tea.
      Please hear me.
You took me as I am:
a mess of a man, gathered by the hands
of Jesus,
son-dried and oxidized now
baptized & optimized for sapid savor.

Flavor was
forced from my frail fibers
while my heart was slowly
steeped in heat deep down like
bold black teas. I call it poetry. These

p r i v a t e

soliloquies once secretly steaming,
now publicly poured-out praise,
aromatic to the nasals of the Ancient of Days.

I'll gladly raise my cup.

And if it's the fire that draws out the best of me
I now know why the kettle sings.

K. PRICE

ANTHOLOGY POET

I'm currently a mother of three children aged 5, 3 and 12 months living in East Texas. Recently, God had lead me on a sanctifying mission of pursuing my family as a homemaker, homeschooling mother, and opening my free time to serve our community and travel as a family.

While I trust Gods plan, this transition has been challenging. I wrote these poems as a way to show how my life is dictated by structure and routine to provide stability and consistency for the little people I'm shepherding, while my dreams and my personality type thrive on spontaneity and adventure.

My life continues to unfold season after season, year after year most unexpectedly, yet I trust this is all leading to my ultimate sanctification in Christlikeness.

 # WHAT IS HOPE?

All humans will undergo trials that they have to overcome, and whether it's more or less extreme, we all seek to grow, resolve and refine in our character as we press through versus letting them overtake us. That light on the other side of our present darkness— that's the hope we all seek.

 # I WRITE BECAUSE...

I write because it's what helps me communicate. My best intentions, pursuits, decisions, and emotional unraveling comes out of writing. It's a gift that I don't take for granted and want to nurture and share with the world.

Glen Rose

Random proverbs pong
around my skull
producing dull
desires growing strong.

Travel - my new favorite song.
Local lands pull
me. Is it wrong
to be so full

from the places I have longed
to be gently lulled
from the quiet? I'm full
from these places I belong.

Covenant

If wedding vows
could write themselves.
In the future, time would tell.

Do you feel
how my palms swell?
I'm hesitant, can you tell?

The security
you want from me,
I can't promise outside
of Our God, Almighty.

I fear this is a sleight of hand-
afraid this vow will crumble to sand.

Dysfunction, my vernacular,
to submit my heart-
that's spectacular.

This aisle's end equals
a checked tax box-
always an option,
never given much thought.

Content in singlehood,
"To thee I do ensnare
my dreams, my desires,"
my heart laid here, bare.

Do you feel
how my palms slip?
One hand on a Bible,
yours, with the other I grip.

"To thee I do wed,"
whether to catastrophe,
I guess we'll grow old and see,
"To thee I do wed,"
God, go before me.

The Art of Mothering

Good morning motherhood!
        Question-
Do you have a peak?
Today, I seek
how to see how this is good-

this season known as motherhood.
I am aware so many meek
have stood,
survived, even- their peaks

of motherhood.
I must be weak
even though I seek
what God says is good-
this opportunity of motherhood.

Notwithstanding

Adventure laying as dormant
as the makeup caking in the bottom drawer.

My mind feels as whittled as
a custom pipe.

I feel as incapable as a calf
born in the winter dew.

Yet, this season fleets
as fast as the lunar day.

I squint to find the good ole' days
as though I need a new prescription.

I shouldn't complain.
I just feel as pointless
as a comma before 'however'.

Jubilee

Why God have you forsaken me?

Where is my year of Jubilee?

I need rest,
for once, not to fight.
Why do you withhold
your might?

My heart is calloused.
My mind is worn,
and God,
I feel like I'm being scorned.

I plead for solace,
I beg for rest.
Have I yet to pass this test?

I wait for freedom I cannot see.
I wait for you- Jubilee.

(She is) Clothed in Baggy Dungarees

(Emphasis by me)
how is she "Clothed in strength and dignity?"

I mean really-
sudsy dishes in the sink,
piles of baby socks missing,
spaghetti sauce dripping,
coffee pot hissing-

She is clothed in strength and dignity?

She walks amongst green board books,
her company completely diaper clad.
Everyday the same-
feed, eat, clean, feed, nap, clean, cook, eat, sleep.

Where does this say
'strong' or 'dignified?'
To me, it's weakness magnified.

Wimberly

To the almost-but-not-quites
who didn't even fully enter my life.

I mourn you two,
the two babies I never knew.

I wince at my lack of sacrifice,
you two fair-skinned children
taught me my true design.

To the almost-but-not-quites,
you'll never knew we inquired about your life.

You never met us, never will,
yet you gave me motivation still.

You two, blond-haired beauts-
the pieces missing I never knew.

You were the almost-but-not-quites,
that I give thanks for unshackling my life.

I mourned the moments that would have been,
had we completely let you in.

Your blue eyes I'm sure light up your new parent's lives.

She Was Devoted –
An Acceptance Speech

I take this moment
lift it up high,

> *("Holy, holy, holy Lord,*
> *God of power and might.")*

recall that day
you opened the heavens wide,

> *("Heaven and earth are full of your glory.*
> *Hosanna in the highest.")*

you gave my blind eyes sight,
woke the Spirit inside,

> *("Blessed is he who comes in the name of the*
> *Lord. Hosanna in the highest.")*

infantile wisdom brings me
to cross where I will die.

> *("Hosanna in the highest.")*

I have neglected my gifts by your design.
Father, I apologize.

("Accept our praises, heavenly Father,
through your Son our Saviour Jesus Christ;
and as we follow his example and obey his com
mand,")

I accept the covenant
to which I've been baptized.

Christ has risen.
Christ had died.

Blessings and honor and glory
to the One up high.

I am devoted, Lord,
my desires, run dry.

JACK MCCLURE
ANTHOLOGY POET

Jack McClure is a Scottish writer and law school graduate with a knack for crafting versed poetry about faith and life experiences.

He aspires to wrap his writing in the encouragement of Christ, for those who need just a bit of hope for tomorrow.

 # WHAT IS HOPE?

"So we fix our eyes not on what is seen, but on what is unseen, since what is seen is temporary, but what is unseen is eternal."

 # I WRITE BECAUSE...

I love the world I live in. Life is beautiful and I like writing about it.

Forgotten Prayer

I've forgotten what I want to say,
I hate my fickle mind!
How can I hope to pray to You
When words, I cannot find.

How can You love someone like me;
Who cannot hold a thought?
My feeble mind cries ever out,
With words, by me, unwrought.

How wonderful it is to me,
Your boundless, binding love,
That fills my heart with gratitude
And sets my mind above.

For even when I cannot pray,
You intercede for me!
I cannot hold a single thought,
Yet You labour on for me!

For every broken word I speak
And every muttered phrase,
The mighty Spirit forever groans
My forgotten prayers in praise.

Thank You Lord for the Holy Spirit,
Who never fails to groan
All my forgotten prayers to You
Before Your eternal throne.

I Look Unto

I look unto that glorious day
That promises rebirth,
When the Lord returns to me,
When the desert becomes earth.

How the wilderness longs for God
And the desert prays to Him.
How they rejoice to see His beloved,
Praising Him with a hymn.

Have courage, oh dear friends of mine,
Be strong and do not fear!
He comes in fury to save us all,
Our debt of sin to clear!

The blind will look unto this day,
The deaf will hear His song.
The lame will leap just like a deer,
The dumb shall sing, with Him, along!

And water will fill the wilderness,
Deserts will flow with streams.
And grass and reeds and rushes will
Grow as the jackal screams.

Nothing holds my gaze like Him,
I look unto His return to me
On the wings of the thunder storm,
He flies to set me free

A Promise

Consecrate this heart of yours unto Me,
For I have chosen, here to dwell,
Where I shall hear your every plea.
I am the Master of rain and well.

Lord of the storm and the locust swarm,
Mine are the keys to Heaven and Hell.
So hark unto My mighty voice, warm
And in all things, seek ye My face.

Wherever I am, and whatever My form,
I will listen and hear in this place.
Every prayer uttered without any fear,
And I will lavish freely, My grace.

As is my want for every prayer I hear,
Uttered in this heart, to Me, so dear.

The Painful Journey of a Rusty Rod

With a bang and a clang
And an explosion of sparks;
Glistening and gliding in twilight
Air, beneath the chirping larks,
He forges me in flames of fire:
A master craftsman, is He.
From a rusty rod to mithril steel,
He shapes and fashions me.
He spends all day hard at work
Bent over His iron anvil,
Swinging His hammer, my lives
Like metal sheets unravel.
With a heave and a ho,
The mighty bellows roar,
Breathing life into dead metal
Like Smaug of Tolkien lore.
With a bang and a clang
He brings me to life again.
Striking off the corrosive rust,
He makes me better through pain.

The Great Blessing

When I am poor with weariness,
Sorrowful for all my sin,
Then I am blessed, for Heaven's gates
Are open for me to go in.

And when I am in mourning for
All those that I have lost;
Then blessed am I to live in hope,
To see them when I've crossed.

When my eyes are fixed to earth,
My care of little worth,
Then I need never be dismayed
For I shall have the earth.

When I am burdened by my sins
And want to do what's right,
Blessed am I for though I fail,
He fills me with delight.

And when I love my enemies
With no earthly reward,
Then great will be His mercy
And love, on me, outpoured.

Though I guard my embattled heart
From sinful lust, adored,

I do not miss out on life, for
I will look upon the Lord.

When the nations writhe and quake
For war that will not cease,
Then I will be a son of God
And live my life for peace.

When I am hunted by my own
For standing, Lord, on You,
Then mine is Your vast Kingdom of Heaven
And I will rest in You.

No matter what is thrown at me,
What demons, against me, arrayed,
In His word, my hope lives on,
I will not be dismayed.

My Hope Remains

My appetite is gone from me, and so
I have no choice but to accept
The gravity that pulls me down below

This world of light, into the sept
And feast with the fiends for a while
As they eat their very souls, inept.

And why, my Lord, through every trial,
Do You persist in loving me?
When every foot feels like a mile

And I cannot, in the darkness, see,
Or comprehend my constant fear
That always seems to conquer me.

Yet, my hope remains, to me, so dear;
Through it all, You are with me here.

Grey Box

I live my life in a grey box with
Worn out carpets on the floor,
Behind my desk, my back to the window,
My eye, ever on the door.

The sunlight ignites the dreary room:
Oh! What a beautiful day.
The door reaches out to take my hand:
Come on out of this lifeless grey.

My legs rev their engines and my
Feet press on the brake.
My heart yearns for the light outside,
But there's money to make.

And as I sit and work and watch,
The room explodes with colour
That lies ever secret and dormant beneath
The veil, grey with lifeless pallor.

All this room needs is the sun to
Restore some light to the blight
And reveal new colour and joy to see;
All one needs in the world is light.

And yet, for all it's dullness and
Sickly pallor, I find
That grey is very much a colour
In my kaleidoscopic mind.

I Am a Creed

I thank the God who saved me,
For with His blood, I am freed.
No more a slave to dying desires,
No more, for I am a Creed.

What are we if we enslave ourselves;
Slaves to our lusts unclean?
All we are, are empty shells,
Dead of desires better unseen.

No more will my appetite dominate me,
I'll abstain from Adam's fruit.
I am the Lord of this ship, my body;
All of it from head to foot.

Like my Lord, I'll live in wisdom
And not by my own desire.
There's more to life than what I want;
More to love than lustful fire.

And so this I vow: to all I'll be true,
For when this world is run by greed
And hope is gone, a pillar, I'll be.
I am not a man. I am a Creed.

Army of One

Hope is a hard thing for us to see
Down in this chaotic place
Of unending war and violence,
In this Paradise we debase.

For all our grief, we are prone to war;
Peace, alone, is not enough.
No matter what we do, how hard we try,
Life finds ways to be tough.

How can one man hope to stand,
With naught but love and grace,
In the face of all that tears us down?
The Devil's legions, we face.

They love nothing more than making
Us feel so pitifully small;
Such weak and feeble little men,
So very far beneath it all.

But I am much more than just a man,
For a universe dwells in me;
A Master of nations of muscle and bone,
My armies of cells inside me.

So like a Lord of many nations,
I stand before it all.
The Devil quakes before my face,
His legions, before me, fall.

For I am more than just a man:
I am a molecular legion.
Atoms and molecules make way for me
For I am an army of One.

Man of No Place

I am a man of no place,
Without a penny to boast:
No fame or fortune to enjoy
And no joy to give a toast.

I am a man of no place,
Tired unto my bones
And all that God can think to give
Are little seeds and stones.

"I built the world with less
Than these, many years before.
I dare you now to build for Me
A world of so much more."

I am a man of no place;
Of little wealth or land.
I take the little that I have
And build with my own hand.

I am a man of no place,
With my seed and stone,
I plant my trees and mountains, tall
And make them all my own.

I am a man of no place,
Where oak grows from a seed,
Where mountains start from little stones
And nature sees to every need.

I am a man of no place;
With my army of trees,
I sit upon my mountain fortress
And do whatever I please.

Guide My Stone

I've always been afraid of giants
Towering over me, they taunt
And sneer, battering me with clubs
And hammers. They ever haunt
My dreams - no, not just dreams -
My thoughts, ugly and gaunt.
Threatening to eat me for lunch,
They lurch forwards and vaunt
On their power and might over me,
Ironically, it's my strength, they want.

What can one do in the face
Of such destruction but make
Such an end as glorious as hope
Will allow? Since all they take,
I cannot rebuild, only return to faith
And start again, trying not to quake
At the rumbling grumble of the earth,
Yielding to their feet; the trees shake.
What can my sticks and stones do
When all in my life is at stake?

I'll keep going, I'll not be afraid,
Even if my body, worn to bone
Cannot move, save to breathe,
I'll never give in for I'm not alone.
I may have naught but a sling
To stop a missile being thrown
Into the mix, destroying all within,
Though my future is yet unknown.
So Lord God, help slay this giant,
Like King David, guide my stone.

CANDACE GREEN
ANTHOLOGY POET

Candace Green is the author of "The Illusion of Fear: How to Live your Best Fear Free Life". She hails from Washington, D.C. and currently resides in Birmingham, AL. She is the current Editor in Chief of iPUSH Foodie Magazine and has written for Femi Magazine and iPUSH Magazine.

She also serves as the Director of Health and Wellness of The Regenerate Society Inc. Candace peels back the curtain in her own life to encourage and uplift others.
When she isn't writing, she's reading (or watching) Game of Thrones, anything Marvel, lifting heavy weights, or trying one of the abundant food choices in Birmingham.

 # WHAT IS HOPE?

Hope is the ultimate culmination of faith. To have hope is to believe in the idea of something. Hope is like the wind. You can't or touch it, but you can feel the impact and see the change it makes.

 # I WRITE BECAUSE...

Writing is my therapy; letters become paint swirling around on a blank canvas. I am thankful to be able to paint beautiful pictures with words.

Where Do Prayers Go?

Our Father, who art in Heaven,
Hallowed be thy name.
Thy Kingdom come, thy will be done
On earth, as it is in heaven.

Where do prayers go?
Is heaven too high that these words can't reach?
Do the words break apart in the wind,
whole words turning into letters?
Do they find their way back together at heaven's door?
Do they get caught in the web of my doubts,
or trapped in my fears?
Do the whispers through my tears make sense,
or the letters that fail to make words in my head?
Does my failing faith block the phone line? Is the mustard
seed the key to unlocking the door?

Where do prayers go?
Are we assigned an imaginary number once we say "amen"?
Are they locked away in a vault at the feet of Jesus?
Wherever they go, there is no place that God can't reach.
In Jesus name, Amen.

Butterflies

It is dark. Very dark. I am warm and wet, and slimy.
I see a very faint light in the distance, and slowly
my eyes start to open.
But I am small
I am very small. So small in fact that I seem to go
unnoticed everywhere I go.
Days pass, and I seem to be growing fast, my eyes drink in
the world around me.
They drink fast, and I seem to have reached a plateau.

It is dark. Very dark. I am warm and wet, and slimy.
I see a very faint light outside in the distance, and slowly my
eyes start to open.
I move toward it, but I am stuck, wrapped in the fear of what
was and what is to come.
I struggle, I struggle hard, but I cannot budge.
I panic, and the air seems to disappear quickly inside the
cocoon.

My energy is spent
and I give up, heavy with failure.
One day I feel different, and I decide to reach the light again.
Small cracks become bigger.
I emerge with wings,
and people tell me my colors are beautiful.

The Wind

Trees sway, weeds roll across the ground
seemingly out of nowhere.
An invisible gust hits your face,
and tears start to fall from the weight of
the invisible gravitational force.
Feet heavy with the weight of our world,
we struggle against it.
Sometimes it stops us in our paths,
an invisible door we aren't allowed to cross.
Yet,
feet stomp, tantrums ensue, why can't I cross?
The harder you push, the more it pushes back.
A light breeze on a hot day,
cooling the sweat beads on our faces
just in time.
Hope is like the wind.

The Apple Seed

A girl planted an apple seed at recess
in the back of her elementary school.
She marked the spot with a bright red "x"
Every day she went to visit with water and a smile.
Every day she saw nothing. Her sorrow was palpable.
Years went by, and nothing was left, not even the red "x"
She left discouraged and confused.
A few years later, the girl visited the school again.
Bright red fruits hung low and heavy on the branches.
A kid ran up to her, pointed to the tree, and asked,
"What is that?"
She replied, "A girl planted an apple seed."

Faded Scars

Snap, crackle, pop!
A bright white light followed by
the smell of burning wood.
Golden flames emerge swiftly and often,
and spread even faster.
Soon she is unable to breathe, and the coughing begins.
The smoke fills the air, her lungs
and she gasps wildly for air
and then she wakes up.
       A huge sigh of relief.

Snap, crackle, pop!
Before she could blink, a slap across her face,
what for, she could never tell.
She reaches up and feels blood running across her cheek and
tastes the saltiness from her tears.
       "What happened to your face?"
         "Oh, I just fell…again."

Everyone knew she was lying, and sympathetic eyes from her
friends unfortunately were not enough.
In time the blood dried, scars faded, and well,
so did she.

Snap, crackle, pop!
More flames, more smoke, more coughing.
However, her lungs got stronger, and instead of stopping, she
was able to make it out.
She held her head high and told her story to anyone who
would listen. The color returned to her cheeks,
and her voice.

The fire had finally faded.

Can Anybody Hear Me?

Can anybody hear me?
Can anybody hear me?
The silence is deafening.
My tears are heavy, falling like boulders
on the shore of my life.
The waves crash against the rocks, and the pile grows.
My voice gets carried away in the wind,
and crashes on the shore.
Can anybody hear me?
I see a light in the distance, but it seems to be still.
My feet are dragging with the weight of my fears,
insecurities, and burdens.
I take another step,
        and another,
                and another,
praying all the while.
The light gets a little closer,
my prayers get a little more fervent.
I finally reach the light, and my tears fall for the last time.
I was finally heard.

If Tears Were Currency

If tears were currency, she was a millionaire.
Morning, noon and night the salty liquid
poured from her eyes.
Another tissue dabbed at the space
where the crease of her eyes meets
and falls onto the floor into the heap.
It is white as the snow falling outside.
The arguments between her parents seem to last as long as
the winter, and it's even icier inside.
More tears, more tissues, and soon her room looks
as if a blizzard fell.

Nobody seemed to notice.

If tears were currency, she was a millionaire.
The snow melted, and so did her resolve.
Her parents had given up it seemed, and although the snow
melted, it was still chilly inside.
Winter was over, outside at least.
A small green shoot emerged from the snow,
green with possibility.
She heard a laugh downstairs, small, but audible.
A smile creeped on her face,
and the salty liquid creeped out once again.
The house felt just a little warmer. Maybe hope had sprung.
If tears were currency, she was a millionaire

The Pool Table

The pool table changed my life.
I'm not sure how it happened, but those familiar routes home
after school became a familiar walk to the
Boys and Girls Club.
I didn't quite fit in at first. Questions rapidly ensued.
"Why are you so quiet?" "What happened to your face?"
I never answered, but they figured it out since the scars never
faded.
In time, the conversation switched.
"8 ball corner pocket!"
Those tournaments became a distraction,
my opponents became my family.
For those few hours, I was alright.
The pool table changed my life.

A Single Barber's Chair

I heard a woman's hair is her crown and glory.
This was the day I lost mine.
I never get picked up early from school.
It was hot that day, and I was coming from recess.
The scene was already ominous, and it looked like I
was in trouble from the other side of the fence.

She didn't say much, and for some reason I didn't ask where
we were going. To this day, I still don't know.
We pulled up and went inside, and there was the
single barber's chair.
Snip, snip, buzz, buzz, and my crown and glory was gone.
"Since you don't want to take care of your hair,
you don't deserve any."
I was 12.
I'm 29, and my crown is still growing back.

She Is Free

Heavy, heavy,
you got so heavy baby,
not from all those cakes and cookies we like to eat
but from the whispers of our doubts, fears and insecurities.
Heavy, heavy,
in the purse she stuffs every morning
with the unrepented sins of yesterday.
Fresh ammo for the enemy's dart gun, right at the target of
her heart.
He hits. Bullseye.
Heavy, heavy.
Is the coffee cup she fills every morning made with
1 part unforgiveness,
1 part impatience,
a dash of jealousy,
and garnished with doubt?
She drinks it quicks as she heads out the door.

Heavy, heavy,
in the car her heart filled with prayer
she feels unworthy to pray.
Why do you feel so far away…God?

Heavy, heavy
are the fears she cries at the altar. She tries to cast her cares on
him, because he cares for me…right?

Heavy, heavy
But then a song came to her heart.
Glory, glory, Hallelujah, since I laid my burdens down.
And that she did. Finally.
Her sins in the sand, washed away by the sea
of forgetfulness.
She was finally free.
Whom the son sets free is free indeed
Oh yes, she is free indeed.

AVG
ANTHOLOGY POET

AVG is a pastor's kid born in Massachusetts and raised in Ohio. Currently exploring the Philly/New Jersey poetry scene, he has written pieces since the 4th grade. The first poem he could remember was a reminder to be true to self before anyone else.

Poetry and writing quickly became tools for self-reflection, expression, and ministry since then. He continues to write because young people have seen themselves in his pieces and began their own creative healing process.

Though he's performed for many years, he still gets nervous because every opportunity is an awesome opportunity!

 # WHAT IS HOPE?

Hope is the anchor that re-centers us when the storms of life tempt us to wander. And even when we do, as did the prodigal son, hope is the thread that tethers us to the One who loves us in our imperfection. It is the mindset that allows patience to see you through to a better version of yourself. It is one of the most powerful superpowers we have.

 # I WRITE BECAUSE...

I write mirrors hoping people see themselves through my poetry; writing is a prism through which people get to explore a more vulnerable spectrum of themselves and unpack the colors that make up the sum of their light.

Hanging
After Billie Holiday's "Strange Fruit"

Another black man was hanged last week.

I would tell you to check out the story
but I too am hanging by a thread
just like you.

Hanging by a 3-fold cord
formed of the following false hopes:

      1. Violence is a cry for help.
      Sing like police sirens in affluent communities;
      and help will arrive swiftly.
      2. Mental health will cease to be a status symbol
someday.
      3. Identity crisis is just a phrase we use when we
need to find ourselves again.

It is at this moment Society wonders:
"What are you complaining about? You got to wake up this
morning!"

Y'all, we got to wake up this morning!
Hanging off the edge of our freedoms,
one hand grappling our humanity,
the other latched to the last rung of a ladder
to whatever tax bracket will satisfy
our hunger!

We got to wake up this morning!
With our sanity held at gunpoint,
strapped in on this roller coaster ride of a life
and we didn't even pay for admission.
Both hands raised 'cause apparently
we ask permission to breathe in these streets.

No! We didn't GET to wake up this morning.
We HAD to.

'Cause Society would sooner squeeze us senseless
than soothe our five senses,

would rather
lace necks with a twisted necklace
pull quickly
and leave rope burns where loved ones' arms should be
would rather bleed these dying bodies empty
than rebuild broken vessels
surely made holy temples.
This society will always leave
an artifact of the hard-knock life.

A black and blue tattoo
of strange fruit
hanging from a family tree.
So naturally,

Society will wonder why we persist.
What could we possibly be hanging on to?

For me, it is a 3-fold cord formed of the following true statements:

>   1. He is familiar with our infirmities.
>   2. He was also hanged and they also put his hands
>   and body up where everyone could see them.
>   3. He said, "If I be lifted up, I will draw humanity
>   unto me."

And because of this fulfilled prophecy,

we can choose
gratitude over grief,
grace over grudges,
victory over violence,
deliverance from depression,
and assurance over anxiety.

So let us prove
what is that good and perfect and acceptable will of God.

To finally free
these strange fruit hanging
from family trees.

The harvest is plenty, but the laborers are few.
Our Master is waiting for your answer.
What will you do?

*but in your hearts honor Christ the Lord as holy, always
being prepared to make a defense to anyone who asks you for
a reason for the hope that is in you; yet do it with gentleness
and respect, - 1 Peter 3:15 ESV*

Beautiful Black Boy

Beautiful black boy.

If they call you animal.
If they do not want you
but watch you like tourists on safari
or try to lock you up like the zoo.

You beautiful black boy, run.

You run with everything you have.
Make them gaze
at your lion's mane,
your cadence, and the weight of your roar.

Make them chase
your lion king swagger,
as you prey on your defining moment.
Make them daze
dumbfounded in the dust
of your pursuit of happiness.

You beautiful black boy, run.

Who could blame you
for establishing your kingdom
after ancestors, held captive,
prayed for your prosperity?
Prayed for the black joy I see
shimmering in your eyes.
Prayed for the black pride you will lead
from the front.
Prayed for the black family
you may already provide for.

Run with your arms wide open
with your eyes fixed on your prize
with your heart extraordinarily full.

You beautiful black boy.

You
beautiful black boy.
You beautiful black boy,
run.

Organs

Father, here I am again.

Wondering if you'll be pleased with my life progressions
When my song finally ends

That when the world presses on my keys
my respiratory organs would pass pneuma through the wind-
pipe of this body
Past my vocal chords and through my lips
whether war cry or whisper
To worship and witness your goodness
with everything it means for me to be breathe
authentic music

Acoustic sounds that are wholly in harmony with your Will

At least, I think that's what it means to be in one accord with
You

But Father, here I am again

Wondering if this heartbeat
still makes you delight in the darkest corners of my confes-
sion
You see
I made a tone meant for sin last night.
Here I am tryna atone for my sin this evening.

But, Father, if this note of apology
outlines the score of my harmony,

do I still strike a chord with you
when I cry, "Lord, have mercy on me,
a sinner"?

I wonder if I can still offer you
children's music ministry,
unadulterated praise
and worship untainted by simulated
musical arrangements...

That I wouldn't autotune myself
just to produce unnatural vibrations.
These "prayers and statements"
audio engineered to sound pretty
But couldn't be farther in beauty
from the natural tones in our humanity.

God,
this is supposed to be a praise poem!

But maybe these cardiac percussions
be the clearest evidence of our humility.

Maybe these,
our most honest heart talks,
be the heartbeats that still make you dance
since the dawn of civilization

when our ancestors
would cut through air to craft choreography
and present as living sacrifice,
a body choir of vibrations
giving Handel's Messiah indigenous twist
and while imperceptible to the human ear,
you heard them.

It was pleasing and acceptable to you
and you alone

So Father, here I am again,
grateful that you hear the honest compositions
of this human heart.

This anthem
outpouring from my ventricles and atria
Into the rest of these organs

May the musings of these four chambers
right now
be our reasonable service.

May this heart chamber music
be concerto somebody's son ought to offer
as symphony.

May these whole notes of authenticity
be the foundation of a heart string quartet

quivering toward its last measure
till its deepest ECHOs delicately vibrate
into silence.

My friends,
what if God just wants to hear us make music
with the organs He gave us?

What if real worship is a style of music
we play so much more so with our bodies
than the instruments we set before them
and the rhythms we set in order?

What if real worship
Is living in harmony with Him and each other?

Would it change how often we give praise?

A King in You

Young man,
give me a moment of your time.

No matter what the world tells you.
No matter what you've been through.
No matter where you are right now.

There is still a king in you.
A leader in you.
A father figure in you.
A steward in you.
A provider in you.
A protector in you.

There is still a higher self in you
and all you have to do
is accept who you are right now.

Set your mind on choosing that inner man
and live out that truth
starting today.

The Queen in You

You make me feel
Like I could be someone

Like I could be King enough
to stand beside
the Queen in you

As many L's as I've taken,
I can't knight my way out of this
I can't escape this perfect square match
Of love and war,
Or bishop to the farthest corners of this earth

I'd happily yell checkmate for you
But I'm not sure you have the fondest clue
How many you empower through
Your story

And right now,
While it may be hard to believe it
You are strategic,

Influential, resourceful,
Street-smart, good book-wise
And I'd perceive your intellectual
Even if you weren't collegiate

In this chessboard of a life,
You are the dream little girls believe in
So please… exude the Queen in you
Whenever you speak an edict

Your voice is needed,

I'm sure you knew that back then
But at some point, you hadn't the fondest clue

Queen, who told you
to exchange your crown?

For a high to leave you
With your head in the clouds
Til you deflate and fall back down
Through the foundation
you used to stand on

Do you not recognize
The worth of being grounded
And stable in your values
This crown
Should never be put down

Remember,
a queen maneuvers
chessboards like she owns the room

So move!

Cause when I see you
You make me feel I could be someone
Like I could be King enough
To stand beside the Queen in you.

Watching a Rose Bloom

"God,
I've seen flowers grow
in graveyards where skeletons
are laid to rest.
So if bones were buried inside me, can I be
made beautiful?"

Miscarriages, family secret
sex partners, or other trauma–
bones
are whatever resonates
with you.

The answer is "yes"
Eve, 'n' you can be made beautiful.
Jesus died in human flesh
'cause you were made beautiful.

You were never a graveyard,
but you are earth in truth.
So I pray seeds are planted
in your heart and mind, your womb.

That you may see how flowers grow
where Death had stolen room.

So as I watch you grow,
I will treat you like a rose,
wear a glove
handle you softly
hold you delicate
careful to respect your boundaries
ready to be taken up by your essence
lifted to a bliss only so many people know

And I hope someday you get to see
just how much you've grown.

Still Standing

Yesterday,
The sun set over the intersection
of yellow-orange and cooler hues of deep blue
as cars traveled in waves like bodies of water,
in ebbs and flows we call traffic as the tragic events
of last year fade
into an ever more distant past

And as dusk approaches,
I notice these cars seem to
Park themselves now
in driveways and beside sidewalks
before humans emerge

Keys… fiddle
locks
turn, knobs twist
and doors
sway open as four walls
welcome sometimes hollow bodies
home

Have you ever asked yourself whether trees make a sound
if they fall when they are home alone?

Cause I don't know about you,
but I was caught slippin'
during quarantine
And I wondered if anybody heard me fall
short of the glory of God

If God himself heard me crack
under the weight of these temptations
Like a law of gravity
working in me to make it seem
like everything that goes up
must come down

If God himself could hear me cry out
for guidance and consistency
As I fell off and on the Rock, Christ Jesus
But it is said

"A righteous man may fall
seven times and rise again"

So even
when the devil took axe to my faith
the Rock
the foundation of everything I believe in
kicked in
And then every breath that I breathed in
declared war against the kingdom that he's leadin'

So I'm still standing

But not on my own merits
I'm standing
On the everlasting arms of a God who loved me
As unlovable as I am

raised me up from six feet of dirt
That I dug myself into
So that I can stand
on the mountains of my past

Of a God who set me
on the shoulders of giant trials
to show me that we are more than conquerors
through Jesus Christ our King

In spite of my past mistakes,
my guilt, and my shame,
I'm still standing
in my faith

It grows
Like a cedar of Lebanon
and it shows
when these limbs
bough themselves
toward the Most High as they bear fruit

So we better not uproot
this growth that He's approved
producing something within us that leaves
His legacy and branches
out further than we ever could...

If you think of your faith like a tree
You may wonder if anyone heard your faith
fall during quarantine

But you did make a sound
You did cry out
and we have not a high priest
who can't be touched
with the feeling of our infirmities

Which means we have a God
who sees with his ears
and listens with his eyes
speaks with His hand
and touches us with His heart

And you may start to wonder, "Why me?!
God, who am I that you are mindful of me?
that my time has not yet come?"

But you must not be deceived

The devil will tell you
"Everything that grows up must come down"
but you are still standing

Even when waves crashed against you
When fallen angels and enemies were stacked against you
No matter how many weapons they craft against you,
You are still standing

So especially when life seems to bring you to your knees
Pray, then rise, give praise
Raise your hands in complete surrender
And render every trial and unresolved situation
to God
Because you could have been

Another tree that will never rise again
But you are still standing

So live
every day
Like you believe it

____

Tomorrow,
The sun will rise over the intersection
of yellow-orange and cooler hues of deep blue
as people travel in waves like bodies of water,
in ebbs and flows we call community as the tragic events
of last year fade
into an ever more present future

And as dusk approaches,
I will notice these people seem to
Be themselves now
as they meet outside
and inside these buildings
before their bodies converge

Keys… fiddle
locks
turn, knobs twist
and doors
sway open as four walls
welcome all but hollow bodies
Home

SAMANTHA M.
ANTHOLOGY POET

Born and raised on the Canadian west coast, Samantha McLauren holds a Bachelor of Arts in Christian Studies/Psychology and enjoys writing as a form of personal expression. What began as a simple poem about the thrilling experience of playing basketball at 13, poetry has become more than a pastime. She values introspection and inspiration and has thus, come to admire "writing on occasion," or whenever the heart so desires. Key themes in her work span from life's loves and losses to discussions of God and her Christian faith. She works in the Christian leadership context and is always excited for new opportunities. In her free time, Samantha is a henna artist, enjoys staying active, and spending time with family and friends.

# WHAT IS HOPE?

As a Christian, hope is found in Jesus Christ. Because of His powerful and redeeming work on the cross, conquering and defeating Death, all creation has hope for a better future- one of human flourishing and shalom. And because God chooses to lovingly partner with humanity as we await Parousia, we share with one another hope we have received from Him, through His sustaining grace, understanding-surpassing peace, and radical love.

# I WRITE BECAUSE...

I write because when I am inspired to write, it is then that I feel most human. Poetry is a safe space for self-expression because I am free to desire, vent about, and explore all of life's unpredictable happenings.

Cynic Made Faithful

is it cynical to be realistic?
For I understand but a smidge
of my gravitating weight of wrongs
yet in the fine line between my individual
perception and conviction
i find a grace overflowing
abounding to take care of me
overcoming self-hate and loving my heart.
For my Saviour has fastened me to His belt
empathizing and vouching for me
at Holy throne
so let it be in faith that i cling
to nothing but
His holy and redeeming love alone.

Freedom Will Reign

a taste of freedom is like a sip of cold water for the parched
desert mouth
it satisfies the embedded desire for liberty
one that is bound to none but a good God
freedom is a gift from God
a glimpse of freedom keeps the eyes
open forevermore
desperate to not miss it
in hopes it shows up again
freedom is sweet yet fleeting at the same time
a sample of freedom leaves the bound
seeking a little more
in a trance they search, unapologetically motivated
freedom in its beauty requires one to yearn for its treasure
its value to the hurting soul
simply, freedom remains
unashamedly coveted until the last day
when all will be free once and for all
when freedom will reign.

Sitting Shiva

sitting cross legged
sadly, strewn upon the circle of your pain
simultaneously sitting within
the depths of hell together
fire and smoke consume us both
tears evaporate as if never there
yet still we sob, joined together
my silence does not betray you,
my dear friend
my action, it comforts
for in solidarity, i am with you
sitting shiva.

True Beloved (an ode of gratitude)

the One for whom this heart beats
i pen this ode:

Lover of my Soul
King of my Heart
You are so gentle with me
taking into careful consideration
defiant doubt and chronic curiosity
You are not rash with me
my unwillingness to trust,
You faithfully transform
with but a small seed of my faith
oh, blessing sprung forth
Giver of my Life
Knower of my Being
You are so patient with me
nudging me forward
You spur me on
to greater things already prepared
answering my prayer, my reason's only plea
for Your will alone- Your glory alone
You are so understanding towards me
So, in confidence do i rest
whilst i consider myself blessed
yes, all thanks to You-
Oh, True Beloved of my Soul!

Dust

mortal confusion, a foolish question
a sincere response, loving instruction
love, in the face of delusion
grace, when our nature denies
He remembers that we are dust.

Theology Student

but i am anything but prudent
my wisdom lies within my depression
without it, i have rootless understanding
of the matchless love of God
and undeniable grace of God
poured out for humanity by Jesus Christ, God Himself
for the study i did, i did in vain
as if to attempt to clean my own stains
but through many a night
the Lord has walked by my side
whilst i was writhing in my weak strength,
grasping onto my precious self made idols,
drenched in the despair of my own knowledge
and gasping for just one last breath of life
He did not leave me alone.
because of His hand holding me,
i have concluded
that though i am the least of these
my little desire makes me a student of faith
tried and tested, refined and renewed
on a daily basis, i am a work in progress
that only He will call into completion
so though i am less in this world,
i am still a student of His,
more than enough for me
a student of Theology.

Grip of Christ

His arm will not tire
nor will His desire end
still, He will hold onto you Dear One
He will remain
when no one else will
for He is your God-
as you are His Beloved
I have known His love to be most true
whilst all alone in the dead of night
so rest assured, He will fight for you
keeping you safe, He will be there.
for such is the strong grip of Christ-
upholding His Dearest,
how He cares
oh, how He cares.

Innate

i believe it is innate
the heart's desire to be free
for it gives meaning to one's existence
allowing them to flourish
by framing those desires in purpose
a freedom that liberates from
expectation, trauma, and worry
freedom is what the heart so naturally desires
but tainted it is, so freedom exists with a cost
one of grave danger until exchanged by kind grace
issued by one God
a heart of stone for a heart of flesh
then only is the human heart made
completely free.

Drifting

slowly and surely i am drifting
away
from the thankfulness of a depraved heart, satisfied
a desperate heart, found belonging
once easily provoked and sensibly broken
now merely nonchalant and almost,
almost indifferent
Your love slips through my fingers
like a mist, it feels like vapour
here and there, once or twice
somewhere in between
but right now, Gracious Saviour,
i ask you, implore you once more
to save me again
empower me once more,
for my flesh is weak
but my Spirit is willing,
please make it more willing.

Blessed Breath

You knit me together in my mother's womb
each stitch so carefully placed, positioned in grace
You meant every part of creation
body, personality, talents and interests
covering me in holy providence
You shielded the developing of my being
from that first moment, small as a kidney
You formed my inmost being
as my heart began to beat in praise
in tune with its Creator, sole Author of life
bearing the mark of Your fingerprints,
i became one of Yours, oh so deeply loved
and with Your approval and blessing
i breathed my first, a human being
a beautiful image created with willful purpose
thank you oh My Father,
first love of my heart
for giving me this life
to You, i owe my blessed breath.

Jesus

let adoration resound
praise arise to reverent heights
overwhelming, all consuming
let hymns of His steadfast love reign
in worship, in awe, in love
let our gratefulness meet His grace
reach His throne
even just to touch the hem of His robe
seated on Majesty's peak
come let us gather at the feet of the Most High
exalted is He
who is worthy of it all
King of the heavens and over all the earth
come let us lift up a song
with everything we have and
with all that we are!

TOLULOPE IBIYODE

ANTHOLOGY POET

Tolulope Ibiyode was born and raised in Nigeria. He currently lives in Ontario, Canada. He started writing poetry in 2018, though he started off writing short raps back in 2008. His writings are centered around social issues, love, technology, faith. He enjoys reading his poems on stage or performing at open mics. A stanza from his poem was mentioned in an article from Toronto Star (Canada's largest online news site).

 # WHAT IS HOPE?

Hope is that conviction that I am not alone in my journeying through life. I am backed by God's power and all things work together for my good, regardless if it doesn't appear as such in the moment

 # I WRITE BECAUSE...

I write to illuminate my world. When I get a revelation in my spirit, I reveal it to the world too, because I believe others can use the message as well.

God for Us

Though the world turn its back against us
Though the sound of war encompass us
God's word says He will always be there for us
He will be there as our refuge and fortress
At His feet, we can drop our burdens - small or huge -
and we'll find rest
This life can be full of trials and tribulations
But in Him, we'll find triumph and jubilation
He never said we won't go through the waters,
if we do, it will not drown us
We might go through fire but we shall not be burned
Be unmoved by what your physical eyes see,
see with the eyes of the spirit
No matter what we might go through in this world,
He said He will never leave us nor forsake us
We can take solace in His promises
Because His Word will forever remain true.

Submission

I often say — Lord, not my Will but Yours
But I still have my two hands on the steering wheel
Instead of You occupying the driver's seat and
taking the lead,
I've always put You in the passenger's seat and
I try to steer You according to my will and desires
I come to you for Nitro boost when I need some speed
or I want an edge
Basically using You as a means to an end
It's clear I'm yet to understand what
submission means
Here I come again, but this time, I'm ready to
turn over a new leaf and put away the old me
Grant me the Spirit of obedience and commitment
That hence, it's Your Will that I'll commit to, till the end.

Fortified

Fought a thousand battles to get here
And I know the end of the battles is not anywhere near
They say, the higher the level, the bigger the devils
But I know I'll always overcome any storm or peril
Because the Word says I was made more than a conqueror
Any weapon fashioned against me, I'll conquer all
Because my strength and protection comes from
the Lord above
Being confident of this very thing,
He that began a good work in me,
He shall see me through -- to the finish line.

Built For This

When the feeling of not being enough kicks in
The one thing you can't afford to do is quitting
When those voices start yelling or whispering...
you were not built for this
You respond with... that might be true for now
but I'm being built in the process and
I will not end it prematurely
You say to you — I'm a winner, not a quitter
No matter the hurdles or oppositions, I will see to it
That I see this through, till I emerge on the winning side
And all that it takes to do so, I am loaded with it -- deep inside.

Empathy

Individually, we are all going through stuff
But somehow the society has conditioned us
to always act tough
When sometimes, all we really need is for
someone to show us some love
I know people that are quick to drag you
they'll say you're acting soft
Like being emotional is not being human!
I know people that would rather suffer in silence
than ask for help and get called weak
More compassion and empathy is what the world needs
People that uplift others, instead of making their heart bleed
And the journey to that kind (of) world begins with me.

Fingerprints

Maybe God made the prints on our fingers unique
As a reminder that we have a unique mark
to make on the world.
While some would impact the world at large
like those who invented the internet or the light bulb,
Some would greatly impact the world of a single person
And that one person would create a ripple effect on others.
As you journey through life,
leave good prints on those you meet
Touch as many as you can with love, kindness and empathy
Bless your world with the unique gifts and abilities you were
blessed with.
You were uniquely made for a reason.

Marathon

A wise man once said to me —
Don't let the person running a sprint
distract you from your own marathon.
Because others have achieved things before you
doesn't mean you are running late or
that you have failed.
Remember, maize and orange don't have the same
growth timeline or life cycle.
Be focused! Face the phase that you are in,
don't allow yourself to be derailed.
In due time (9 months, maybe more, maybe less),
all that you've been laboring for would be birthed,
just don't stop pushing, it would all be worth it in the end.

Shine

You've doubted your gifts
You've questioned your skills
You've quieted your heart

But have you considered doubting your doubts
You know that voice that tells you—
you aren't as good as you think you are
It even asks you—who do you think you are!

Maybe it's time to reaffirm that
you are a super-duper star
That you were placed on this Earth to shine
And you'll perpetually and ever-increasingly
shine your light — unstoppably!

Precious Gift

A wise man once said to me
You can't live your best life dwelling on the past
Leave the hurts behind but take the lessons
with you, as tools in your toolbox
What doesn't kill you oftentimes leaves you
more equipped.

If all you think about is the future, you can't
fully enjoy the now
And this moment is a gift, embrace the present
To no one is tomorrow is guaranteed,
(it doesn't mean you shouldn't plan for it)
The past is gone, the future isn't here,
now is the only time that truly exists.

Mirror

When you look in the mirror, what do you see?
The person who God made; wonderful and beautiful
Or the person who the society has re-defined?
Words become obsolete when we stop using them
In the same way, you start losing yourself when you
stop seeing your true self (the person who God made)
Never let the society take away your identity
You are too simple and too complex
for them to comprehend
And people often misjudge what they can't understand
Be unmoved, stay true to you,
be you to the full (beautiful)
Be who God made you to be; a reflection of Him.

IFEOMA OGBONNAYA
ANTHOLOGY POET

Ifeoma is a creative writer with a passion for expressing the gospel through poetry. She writes free verse poems that inspire people to persevere through difficult moments with hope, courage, and faith in God. Her writing style incorporates simplicity which makes it open and easily relatable.

 # WHAT IS HOPE?

Hope is the belief that things eventually work out for your good.

 # I WRITE BECAUSE...

I believe that our words are powerful enough to inspire life-changing outcomes.

Abba's Own

The man whose heart looks to You
abides in peace undefiled.
Even when it seems like storms linger
I know there are quiet pastures approaching.

Quiet pastures - where I can lean into the arms
of my loving Father.

I am ABBA's own.
This is my song when turbulent noise surrounds me.
He cares for me.
He has not forgotten that He made me.

The man whose heart looks to You
is filled with hope
for He knows that He has a future.
A future planned by the Father who wants him well.

So I look to You ABBA
because You know my name.
Your thoughts are good and Your promises true.
My heart is stayed on You and in perfect peace You keep me.

Armour

Darkness brings his weapons
and fear tries to follow.
Lies upon lies the enemy tells
"The race is not to the swift
so you'll never win" - he scoffs

he brags about his conquest and claims the victory,
he's always trying to disprove what God has said.
Twisting and turning he tries to cast a doubt
but this time, I'm not unprepared.

The word of God is my armour
so I'm not an easy prey.
I know that He won this fight through Christ Jesus.
He disarmed the powers of darkness
and put them to an open shame,
triumphing over them for good.

Now, I can stand against the enemy's wiles.
his evil schemes and deceit
I see as they really are.

In Christ, I am victorious.
Not wavering in hope or strength
because the word of God is my defence.

Stay

Time is fleeting, that's how it feels.
It's easy to miss a step while seeking,
trying to get a grip as the cares of life come like a flood.

I want to run with the wind.
Gliding upon her tides
and swaying as she beckons
but You tell me to stay.

Waiting is hard,
for times and seasons are always passing.

I tend to forget who is in control
so I let my thoughts wander
and open up doors to anxious calls.
But through it all, I hear Your voice.

You remind me,
that they who wait on You
shall be made strong.
Mounting upon wings as eagles
they run without limit.
Standing tall like an edifice
they will not faint.

So though waiting may be hard sometimes
I know that You guide me,
Your voice leads me
and with Your word in my heart,
I stand upon the assurance
that You are with me.

Preservation

These days brim with contradictions,
but we look to the Lord for His preservation
in a world that bears the brunt of self-destruction,
We do not hold on to what is temporal.

Drawing from ABBA's fountain
we march on as we proclaim God's goodness.
We see the gospel prevail
and more men embrace salvation.
God's mighty power shall keep us.

We do not slack in devotion
but hold on to this profession of faith,
for earnest expectations
bring forth the miraculous.

If you ever have a worry,
remember that God works in you.
He'll keep you from falling.
He'll perfect what He started.

So look on beloved.
Look to the Father.
Look to the Son.
Let the Holy Spirit guide you
until the day He returns.

Onward

Pressing on, I see all that lies before me
in the light of what You have spoken.
Your promises that never fail
and Your word that's unbreakable.

Marching on, I sing victory songs,
rhythms You pour into my heart
and melodies brewed within my Spirit.
There's comfort even when chaos looms.

Moving on, I keep in view the visions You present
I know You are faithful to perform all that You say.

This is my delight, knowing that You are with me.
You are for me, and Your strength is all that I need.

Stagger Not

When days birth weeks
and lonely seasons fail to fade,
I'll trust your way and seek your face

for the one who looks to You
is sure to find a safe abode.

Though the tempest rises
my heart will find its peace with You.
I'll stagger not at the promises You made.

My faith is alive,
the substance to this hope that I have in You.

When it seems like the fight is lost
and my defences fall in shards,
I'll cling to Your word and sing Your praise.

I'll arise with glorious chants
for You, O'Lord are on my side.

I'll lift my voice above
all the storms that may come,
knowing that my Father is Lord over all.

Faithful God

Comfort comes to the weary man
If he will lay his fears aside
and seek the Lord who cares for Him

Life presents many trials
and we may not know what battle comes next
But if we stay with the Lord who knows all things
We'll have a sure guide through the troubles that come

God is faithful.
With eyes that never sleep
He'll watch over His own.
With arms stretched out
He'll make a way

Our job is to trust Him
To lay aside our fears and worries
To lay up worship in His presence
To delight in the love He pours out
And to embrace the peace He freely gives

Walk on Water

Our minds sometimes drift from the vision
God has placed in our hearts,
So we wonder if they'll ever be.

Our eyes only see the mountains
and the oceans in between,
So we choose to hide from purpose.

But the Father beckons,
He wants to take us by the hand
and lead us to the promise He has made.

He laid the vision before us
so that we may eagerly press on
even when the odds try to fight us

It is ours to believe
that He is able to complete
the good work which He began

To take a faith leap upon the oceans,
knowing that He is with us
as much as He is ahead of us,

To keep our gaze upon
the Father who loves us
and has called us by His name.

The Witness

To see rivers in deserts
and plain lands where mountains stand
Is a witness that the Lord has gone ahead of us

To sing high praises and lift victorious hands
when adversaries approach
Is a witness that the Lord fights for us

To lay up gold
and gather treasures in parched lands
Is a witness that the Lord is providential

Surely, our hearts will always know God's goodness
And our souls will take pleasure in His faithfulness
That we may wait upon Him without a doubt
And align with His plans at every step

That we may gather strength
and prevail over storms because the Lord our God is true.

Blessed of the Lord

I am unshaken
a city set by the Lord
and a flourishing tree by the riverside.

I am unperturbed,
abiding in my Fathers love
and living in His will.

I am strong,
strengthened by His Spirit within
and empowered to live in the sufficiency of God's grace.

I am loved,
I thrive in the land that God has given to me
and lay in pastures He has prepared for me
like a field blessed by the Lord, I bear fruit.

I am a child of the true King,
living daily in high authority through Christ Jesus.

ERINMA CHUKWUKA
ANTHOLOGY POET

Erinma Chukwuka is a Nigerian Christian writer, poet and spoken word artist. She has recently published her first collection titled "Just Words" which is now available online to all her readers.

When she's not writing, you can find her on Instagram where she posts daily inspiration Christian poems and shining the light of truth in her corner of the social media world.

 # WHAT IS HOPE?

Is the conviction I have in God that all my expectations will be met. It gives me the strength I need to wake up every morning and face the day with a smile because like the Bible says,
"Joy comes in the morning."

 # I WRITE BECAUSE...

What started as a thing of curiosity became a hobby then a passion. I can't find myself not writing, so long as God keeps dropping His words in my heart, I am going to keep on writing.

Hope Remains

Hope remains,
a tale I've been told
a thousand times over
but seem never to comprehend.

Why would all my foes prosper?
How about my unmet desires?
Yet, you whisper
 "Hope remains?"

Its dark and cold,
the northern wind
sings terror.

But in the rustling of the leaves
 of the willow tree,
I hear a familiar song I once forgot,
it's a song of joy
and possibly of praise
even in these times.
The willow tree bends and turns
but never falls.

Suddenly the night sky clears
and the northern wind quietens
to a complete halt
and now the sun in all its glory
shines above me
and a new found warmth fills my heart.

"For everything, there is a season..."
I hear in the gentle breeze
that now blows around me,
Is the voice of the One who saved me,
Who I once called "Abba Father"
His voice has been faint,
But now,
His voice
is as clear as the sun
that shines above my head.

Yes,
finally I agree,
"Hope still remains."

Ashes

I've heard
that from the ashes,
rises the phoenix.

Quite strange,
don't you think?
How this coincides
with the intricacies of our life
and all its tales?

Once down,
low in the dust
succumbed to the state of mere ashes,
He,
the creator of our souls,
God of all,
came forth
and breathed upon us
in our state of weakness
and now we live,
soaring high like the phoenix.

Does Love Die?

Does love die?
in the wait of time,
meticulously searching
for an approval at sight?

Yes,
we must be fair to each other
and say the truth,
especially when we see it in plain sight.

We are caught up
in a world,
who knows nothing
other than its own,
with twists and turns
but ends up falling
in the same spot.

We are doomed,
I guess?
To follow
in the world's ways
because the world
is the place
we stay.

Well what if I say
that there's
another way?
Yes,
with straight,
clear paths
and fulfilled
hopes and desires
and best
Love never dies!

It's the way of the cross
I'm told,
it's a little bit old
but I heard you can lay
all your cares there
and they would all go away,
all the pain,
worries and fear
will all disappear
like they were never there
and instantly
you will be filled with a love
that truly never dies.

Seeds of Hope

One step at a time,
let the seeds rise
to a mighty plant,
it will only take just a matter of time.

You may not know
but what coincides
with faith and joy,
is the way of hope itself.

Things don't look well,
everywhere seems
dark and weary
but tiny bits of hope
does create holes
for little rays of light
to seep through
and with those,
one day we will see
the full light of day
but those seeds
needs to be planted,
little seeds of hope,
one day at a time
till its a mighty plant
rising high to the sun
when we see the light of day.

Dark Halls

Dark halls,
they are filled
with pain and fear,
looming around the dark,
bellowing scary echoes
that chills one to the bone.

I've been there,
not the best place to be
and the thing is,
even if you loathe it,
to be a current visitor to these dark halls,
can be a normal occurrence.

At times you feel
you're bright and high,
ready to face the world
and all that goes,
but the next second,
you're singing your blues
within the dark halls.

Like I said,
I've been there
and it really wasn't the best place to be,
until I stopped hoping on me,
my strength
and all I could be,
Instead I started to look up at the Lord
cause He alone
is able and more
to do all He ever promised,
one of which is
my end
will be glorious
and the enemy
I will surely defeat.

Then,
little by little,
my constant visit
to the dark halls
became shortened
until it reached a final halt
and now only joy is my constant visitor.

Thank you for reading "Our Hope Remains Vol. 1"

We sincerely hope this collection has encouraged and inspired you to walk forward, take a chance, and remember that hope is universal. From Africa, to America, Canada and Europe, each poet describes what steadfast hope in Jesus Christ is in the midst of uncertainty.

At this moment, we'd like to turn our eyes to 2 Corinthians 1:3-4 ESV which states:

"Blessed be the God and Father of our Lord Jesus Christ, the Father of mercies and God of all comfort, who comforts us in all our affliction, so that we may be able to comfort those who are in any affliction, with the comfort with which we ourselves are comforted by God."

To Him be all the glory, the maker of all things and giver of life in all circumstances.

Our Hope Remains.

You can discover more on the poets listed at the following resources:

Edward Holmes - www.edwardlholmes.com
Published Poetry: "Bravery & Brevity"
"Fingerprints of Love & War."
Childrens Books: "I Can Be Pretty"
Instagram: @edwardlee_on_ig

K. Price - wildlyrootedministry.org
Published Poetry: "Sown"
Instagram: @mama_k_price

Erinma Chukwuka
Published Poetry: "Just Words"

Candace Green - www.candacegreen.com
Non-Fiction: "The Illusion of Fear"
Instagram: @c_dog93

AVG
Published Poetry: "Love, God" "Things I Wish I Said"
Instagram @just_above.avg_

Tolulope Ibiyode
Instagram: @gods1son_

Ifeoma Ogbonnaya
Published Poetry: "The Gospel In Poetry"
Instagram: @content_agenda

Jack McClure
Instagram: @thequaintsaint